AF226046

YOGA ME

Written by
Dr. Daniela Maddern-Leserer

Illustrated by
Jane Harbison

A Daniela Maddern-Leserer Publication
Dr. Daniela Maddern-Leserer,
Copyright ©2024 All rights reserved.

Cataloguing-in-Publication data is available from the
National Library of (USA) I SBN: 9781917438117
Printed in (USA)

Written by: Dr. Daniela Maddern-Leserer
Illustrated by: Jane Harbison

In the middle of a pandemic, I had the great experience of reading Dr. Daniela Maddern-Leserer's book Yoga Me. As a clinician, I am moved by Yoga Me, it is a powerful tool for healing. Dr. Maddern-Leserer presents this work in a way that is accessible and easy to use. What a gift to be able to locate our emotions in our body through yoga, something so needed in our world today. Yoga Me is one of the best antidotes to the pandemic that I have come across. My dream is that this book will be integrated into online learning for children during these times of uncertainty.

Frank Buckley, PsyD., S.J.

Yoga Me is a beautiful meditation on better understanding, experiencing, and working through our emotions. Exquisitely written and gracefully illustrated, this book inspires the reader toward fuller and deeper expression of their emotional life, while masterfully guiding them through poses and exercises that help center and stabilize, creating inner peace and balance.

Adam Rodriguez, PsyD

breathe in breathe out

Contents

AnGER

Loud and scary like a bear,

You definitely know when it is there.

Red and hot – you want to scream

Fast, just like a lightning beam.

Balloon Breath

Lie on your back on the earth with your hands on your belly.
Close your eyes if you wish.
Slowly inhale through your nose, filling your belly up with air.
Then let the air out, breathe out through your mouth, making
a sound like air escaping from a balloon.

Lion's Breath

Sit on your knees and frame your face with your hands – spread your fingers. Now take a deep breath in, and then open your mouth wide and stretch your tongue out, open your eyes wide and let your breath (and anger) out while making a "haaaaaaa" sound.
Roar like a lion.

Wood Chopper

Stand tall, feet apart, and grounded firmly into the earth.
Inhale, take the arms up over the head. Exhale swing the arms down
and back behind you as you squat, keeping the heels on the floor.
Let it all out!

breathe in breathe out

"Yoga helps me release my anger."

breathe in breathe out

JOY

Free and blissful, soaring high,
Like a butterfly dancing in the sky.
Sending love to every girl and boy,
And hoping their hearts are filled with joy.

Butterfly

Sit on the earth and allow the soles of your feet to gently touch each other. Straighten your back and ground your legs into the earth, now move your knees gently up and down; let the butterfly fly. What color is your butterfly?

Seed to Flower

Make yourself small like a seed on the floor (standing on your feet and kneeling down with your arms wrapped around your knees) and then slowly rise up and stand up with your hands in the air like a flower.

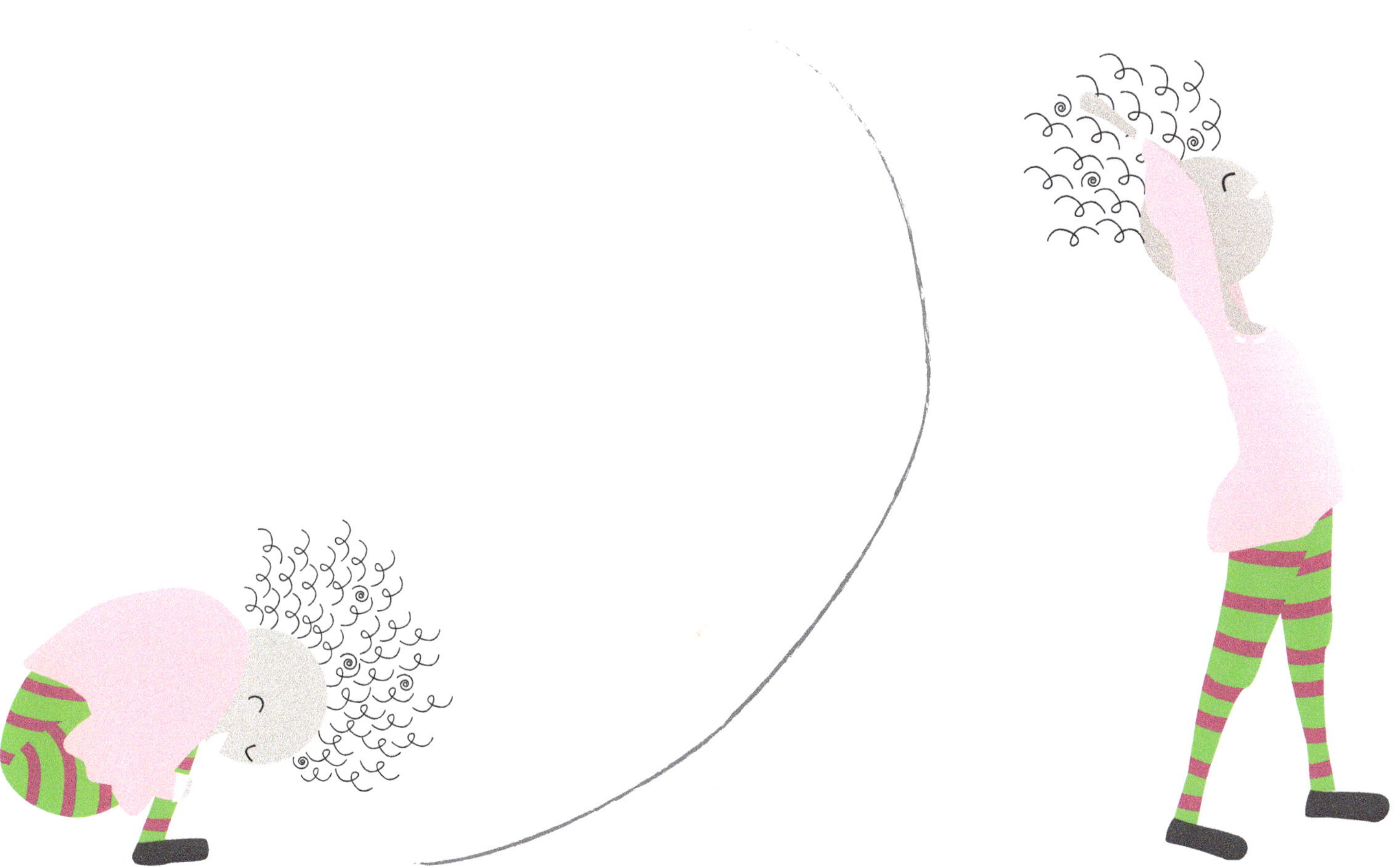

Cat/Cow

Start in tabletop position, hands and knees on the ground. Now, with a deep breath in, curl your back up, scoop your tummy in like a cat, and look towards your tummy. Meow like a cat.

Then curl your spine, move your sacrum up, and look to the heavens. Mooooo like a cow.

breathe in breathe out

"Yoga helps me celebrate my joy."

breathe in breathe out

You can feel it in your heart,
It is painful, piercing like a dart.
You feel heavy, dark and small,
and want to roll up in a ball.

Downward Dog

Start on your hands and knees, then with an in-breath, lift your hips in the air while pressing down heels and palms. Look between your legs.
You can also lift one leg and then the other for three legged dog pose.

Breathe. Change your view.

Snake

Lie with your belly on the floor. Press the tops of the feet firmly into the floor and on an inhale, begin to straighten the arms to lift the chest off the floor. Make a hissing sound: sssshhhhh.

Superman/Superwoman

Start on your hands and knees, now extend your legs back while keeping your hips up. Keep your body in a straight line from head to toes.

Breathe. You are amazing!

"Yoga helps me to open my heart."

FEAR

Fear is described best,
Like a horse galloping in your
chest.
Sweaty palms, eyes open wide
I want to run away and hide.

Warrior I "I am Strong"

Stand on top of your mat, step the right foot to the back, turning your toes slightly outward, then bend your left leg, making sure the knee does not fall over the ankle. Lift your arms up overhead and focus on one point in front of you. Your are a warrior. Breathe in and out and affirm yourself: "I am strong."

Now repeat on the other side.

Warrior II "I can do it"

From warrior I pose with the left leg at the back of your mat, extend your arms parallel to the earth.
Your body is now turned to the side, look over your right arm. You are a warrior.
Affirm yourself: "I can do it."

Now repeat on the other side.

Bird

Stand tall, lean forward, extend your arms to the sides and one leg to the back. Focus on one point to keep your balance. Affirm yourself: "I am free."

Now repeat on the other side.

breathe in breathe out

"Yoga helps me face my fears."

breathe in breathe out

CaLM

Light & soft, just like a cloud,
My body is still, my breathing seems loud.
I rest my body, and am thankful to be,
Still and calm and simply just 'me'.

Tree

While standing on the earth, lift one foot up and place the sole of the foot on your upper thigh; you can now extend your arms overhead and imagine your arms growing like branches. You can also hold on to the wall for some more stability.

Focus your eyes on one point in front of you and hold your gaze.

Breathe. You are sturdy and calm.

Bee

Start by kneeling on the earth, now lean forward and reach your arms alongside your body, breath in and with your out breath make the sound of a "beeeeeeeeeeeee".

Repeat three times.

Cloud

Lie down on your back, legs and arms extended by your body, palms facing up. Close your eyes and imagine sinking into a cloud. Peacefully being carried by a soft, white cloud, quiet and calm. Let your breath come naturally.

Be you.

"Yoga helps me relax."

breathe in

breathe out

Dr. Daniela Maddern-Leserer is a Clinical Psychologist, author, business owner, and an enthusiastic Yogi. She is a mommy to three beautiful children. She is also a children's yoga teacher and teaches her classes in English and German. Her dream is that more children learn from a very young age to be mindful of their emotions and learn to master and enjoy them. This book is meant to be a step towards that dream.

Jane Harbison is a designer, author, and business owner. She grew up in rural Australia and now lives on the Brisbane River with her beautiful husband and son. Jane is passionate about creativity and children having the confidence to master the process of it. When they do, they can take on any problem with originality and calm. This book is a beautiful companion for doing just that.

ANGER

JOY

CALM

SAD

FEAR